MW00882008

RUTH HOLEWINSKI

The Right Words for School Administrators

Words of Praise, Support, Appreciation and More

Copyright © 2024 by RUTH HOLEWINSKI

All rights reserved. No part of this publication may be reproduced, stored or transmitted in any form or by any means, electronic, mechanical, photocopying, recording, scanning, or otherwise without written permission from the publisher. It is illegal to copy this book, post it to a website, or distribute it by any other means without permission.

However, the author grants permission to individuals using this book for its intended purpose: to communicate words of praise and appreciation to faculty, staff, volunteers, vendors and others with whom they have a professional relationship.

First edition

This book was professionally typeset on Reedsy.
Find out more at reedsy.com

To my two favorite school administrators of all time,
Ed Wilson and Theresa Sparks.

My late father, Ed Wilson, was a distinguished leader
in his school district and an exceptional father.
His dedication and passion for education
continue to inspire me every day.

Theresa Sparks serves as a regional director in the
Catholic School Department of the Diocese of Sacramento, CA.
My husband and I are among her many enthusiastic supporters
admiring her commitment to excellence in education.

Contents

Preface

If I'm writing a series of books to help individuals find just the right words to communicate, then naturally, I'd include "The Right Words for School Administrators." Following the release of "The Right Words for Educators," this book is a continuation of my commitment to supporting those in the education field.

As the child of a high school English teacher and a school administrator, I learned early on the importance of making a teacher's life easier. My mother instilled in me the value of being a supportive student and, later, a supportive school parent. Through these books, I continue my mission to uplift and assist those who play vital roles in our educational system.

School administrators face a uniquely challenging role in the dynamic and ever-evolving world of education. From fostering a positive school culture to addressing the diverse needs of students, teachers, staff, vendors, school boards and volunteers, administrators must wear many hats. At the heart of successful administration is effective communication. The right words at the right time can significantly impact morale, motivation and the overall school environment.

"The Right Words for School Administrators" is written to provide you with thoughtful phrases and expressions to articulate appreciation and build stronger relationships with everyone in the school community.

This book reflects my deep respect and admiration for the educators and administrators who dedicate their lives to shaping young minds and fostering educational excellence. By equipping you with the right words, I hope to make your challenging job a little easier and even more rewarding.

Thank you for your commitment to education and for making a difference in the lives of countless students. May this book serve as a valuable resource in your daily endeavors.

Introduction

As an administrator, you know that words of praise and recognition can significantly impact the morale and motivation of those who contribute to the success of a school. From teachers and staff to vendors, school boards, and volunteers, each individual plays a crucial role in creating a thriving educational environment. This book is designed to help you find just the right words to acknowledge and celebrate their efforts.

In these pages, you'll find carefully curated lists of words and phrases that you can use to express gratitude and admiration for the diverse contributions made by each group. Whether you're commending a teacher's dedication, recognizing a staff member's hard work, appreciating a vendor's reliable service, honoring the strategic guidance of school board members or celebrating the selfless efforts of volunteers, this book will provide you with the perfect words to convey your appreciation in a brief note.

By using the right words, you can foster a culture of recognition and positivity within your school, inspiring everyone to continue striving for excellence. Let this book be your go-to guide for crafting heartfelt and meaningful messages that honor the invaluable contributions of all those who make your school a place of learning and growth.

FACULTY

Words of praise from the administrator to the teachers are a testament to their hard work and dedication. These acknowledgments show that their efforts do not go unnoticed. Typically, it's the teachers who provide feedback and guidance to students and communicate with parents. It's truly validating to be recognized and appreciated for one's contributions.

1. **Classroom Innovation:** Your innovative teaching methods keep our curriculum engaging and relevant. Students are always excited to attend your classes. Keep up the fantastic work!

2. **Student Mentorship:** Your dedication to mentoring students is truly inspiring. You help guide them not only academically but also in their personal growth. Thank you for making such a positive impact.

3. **Professional Growth:** Your commitment to professional development is commendable. You are always seeking new ways to improve and it shows in your teaching. Keep striving for excellence!

4. **Classroom Atmosphere:** Your classroom is always a welcoming and positive space. Students feel safe and

valued, which enhances their learning experience. Thank you for creating such a nurturing environment.

5. **Collaborative Spirit:** Your willingness to collaborate with your colleagues strengthens our school community. Your teamwork and support are greatly appreciated. Keep fostering this collaborative spirit!

6. **Parent Engagement:** Your proactive communication with parents is exceptional. It builds strong partnerships that support student success. Thank you for keeping parents so well-informed and involved.

7. **Student Motivation:** Your ability to motivate students is remarkable. You inspire them to strive for their best in all they do. Keep being such an encouraging force!

8. **Adaptability:** Your adaptability to different teaching situations is impressive. You handle changes and challenges with grace and maintain a focus on student learning. Thank you for your flexibility.

9. **Student Support:** Your dedication to supporting students beyond academics is commendable. You care deeply about their well-being and it shows. Keep fostering their social-emotional development.

10. **Creative Lesson Planning:** Your creativity in lesson planning keeps students engaged and excited about learning. You bring subjects to life in unique and interesting ways. You're doing fantastic work!

11. **Equity and Inclusion:** Your commitment to equity and inclusion ensures all students feel valued and supported. You promote a classroom environment where diversity is celebrated. Thank you for upholding these important values.

12. **Professionalism:** Your professionalism sets a high stan-

dard for our school community. You handle challenges with integrity and positivity. Thank you for being such a reliable and positive role model.

13. **Positive Reinforcement:** Your use of positive reinforcement motivates students to achieve their best. You celebrate their successes and encourage continuous growth. Keep up the excellent work!

14. **Cultural Sensitivity:** Your awareness and respect for cultural diversity enriches our school community. You incorporate diverse perspectives into your teaching. Thank you for promoting cultural sensitivity.

15. **Community Involvement:** Your efforts to engage with the broader community strengthen our school's ties. You foster partnerships that benefit our students and families. Thank you for your community engagement.

16. **Classroom Organization:** Your well-organized classroom environment facilitates effective learning. Students know what to expect and this supports their success. Keep maintaining this level of organization!

17. **Extracurricular Leadership:** Your leadership in organizing extracurricular activities enriches students' experiences beyond the classroom. You provide opportunities for growth and enrichment. Thank you for your dedication.

18. **Parent Involvement:** Your encouragement of parent involvement positively impacts student achievement. Families feel welcomed and valued in our school community. Thank you for fostering these important connections.

19. **Reflective Practice:** Your commitment to reflective practice enhances your teaching. You continually seek to improve and adapt your methods. Thank you for your

dedication to continuous improvement.

20. **Role Model:** Your role as a positive influence on students and colleagues is invaluable. You exemplify integrity, kindness, and dedication. Thank you for being a role model in our school community.

21. **Positive Classroom Culture:** Your efforts to cultivate a positive classroom culture are appreciated. Students thrive in an atmosphere of respect and inclusivity. Thank you for creating such a nurturing environment.

22. **Data-Driven Instruction:** Your use of data to inform instruction ensures targeted support for student growth. You analyze progress effectively and adjust teaching strategies accordingly. Keep up the excellent work!

23. **Mentorship:** Your role as a mentor to newer teachers is invaluable. You provide guidance and support that positively impacts their professional growth. Thank you for your mentorship.

24. **Student-Centered Approach:** Your commitment to a student-centered approach in teaching ensures that the needs and interests of our learners are at the forefront of your instructional decisions. Thank you for putting students first.

25. **Technology Integration:** Your effective integration of technology enhances student learning experiences. You use digital tools to enrich lessons and promote 21st-century skills. Thank you for embracing technology in your teaching.

26. **Creativity in Assessment:** Your innovative assessment methods provide valuable insights into student learning and growth. You use assessment as a tool for improvement. Thank you for your creative approach.

27. **Positive Attitude:** Your positive attitude towards teaching is contagious. You approach each day with enthusiasm and a can-do spirit. Thank you for your wonderful energy!

28. **Student Engagement:** Your dedication to keeping students engaged in lessons is evident. You find creative ways to make learning meaningful and enjoyable. Keep up the fantastic work!

29. **Commitment to Excellence:** Your commitment to excellence is evident in everything you do. You strive to provide the best possible education for your students. Thank you for setting such a high standard.

30. **Resilience:** Your resilience and determination during challenging times inspire confidence and unity among colleagues and students alike. Thank you for your unwavering commitment.

31. **Leadership in Curriculum Development:** Your leadership in curriculum development has greatly benefited our school. Your innovative ideas and dedication to improvement are truly appreciated. Keep leading the way!

32. **Student Relationships:** Your ability to build strong, positive relationships with students makes a huge difference in their lives. They know they can trust and rely on you. Thank you for being such a supportive figure.

33. **Cultural Awareness:** Your cultural awareness and sensitivity enhance our school's inclusivity. You make sure every student feels seen and valued. Thank you for your commitment to diversity.

34. **Continuous Learning:** Your dedication to lifelong learning is truly inspiring. You continually seek out new knowledge and skills to improve your teaching. Keep up the amazing work!

35. **Supportive Colleague:** Your support for your colleagues is invaluable. You are always there to lend a helping hand or a listening ear. Thank you for being such a great team player.

36. **Positive Classroom Environment:** Your efforts to create a positive classroom environment are evident. Students feel safe and respected, which enhances their learning experience. Thank you for fostering such a positive space.

37. **Effective Communication:** Your clear and effective communication with students, parents and colleagues strengthens relationships and promotes a positive school culture. Thank you for your excellent communication skills.

38. **Celebration of Achievements:** Your recognition and celebration of student achievements motivates them to strive for their best. You create an environment where success is acknowledged and celebrated. Thank you for highlighting their accomplishments.

39. **Civic Engagement:** Your efforts to engage students in civic activities and discussions are commendable. You help them become informed and active citizens. Thank you for promoting civic awareness.

40. **Mentor to Students:** Your role as a mentor to students goes beyond academics. You guide them in their personal growth and development. Thank you for being such a positive influence.

41. **Creative Problem-Solving:** Your creative problem-solving skills enhance our school's ability to address challenges. You think outside the box and find effective solutions. Thank you for your innovative thinking.

42. **Dedication to Inclusivity:** Your dedication to inclusivity ensures that all students feel welcome and valued. You go above and beyond to create an inclusive classroom environment. Thank you for your commitment.

43. **Positive Reinforcement:** Your use of positive reinforcement motivates students to strive for excellence. You celebrate their achievements and encourage continued growth. Keep up the excellent work!

44. **Student Advocacy:** Your advocacy for students' needs ensures they receive the support necessary for their academic and personal growth. Thank you for prioritizing their well-being.

45. **Collaborative Projects:** Your leadership in collaborative projects enriches our school community. You bring people together to work towards common goals. Thank you for your collaborative spirit.

46. **Role Model for Students:** Your role as a positive role model influences students and colleagues alike. You exemplify integrity, kindness, and dedication. Thank you for being a role model in our school community.

47. **Student Engagement in Extracurriculars:** Your dedication to engaging students in extracurricular activities provides them with valuable experiences beyond the classroom. Thank you for your commitment.

48. **Classroom Innovation:** Your innovative teaching methods keep our curriculum engaging and relevant. Students are always excited to attend your classes. Keep up the fantastic work!

49. **Professional Commitment:** Your unwavering commitment to the education profession and our school's mission makes a significant difference in the lives of our students.

Thank you for your dedication.

50. **Overall Impact:** Your passion, dedication and positive impact on our school community are deeply appreciated. Thank you for your continued commitment to excellence in education.

PARAPROFESSIONALS

Words of praise from the administrator are an acknowledgment of paraprofessionals' exceptional work. These words signify that their efforts are valued and noticed. While it's the teachers who design the lesson plans, these individuals assist them by helping in the classroom and beyond. Recognition for their contributions will be deeply appreciated.

1. **Classroom Management**: Your classroom management skills are exceptional. You help maintain a structured and positive learning environment under the teacher's supervision. Keep up the outstanding support!
2. **Student Engagement**: Your ability to engage students in meaningful activities is impressive. You assist the teacher in making learning fun and interactive. Keep inspiring our students!
3. **Adaptability**: Your adaptability in diverse situations is commendable. You handle changes and challenges with grace, supporting both students and teachers effectively. Keep being flexible and resilient!
4. **Collaboration**: Your collaborative spirit enhances the educational experience. You work seamlessly with teach-

ers to support student learning. Keep fostering that teamwork!

5. **Communication**: Your communication skills are top-notch. You convey information clearly and effectively, helping students understand their tasks. Keep up the great communication!

6. **Creativity**: Your creativity in supporting lesson plans is remarkable. You bring fresh, innovative ideas to the classroom. Keep inspiring with your creativity!

7. **Dependability**: Your reliability is truly appreciated. You consistently show up ready to support and assist both teachers and students. Keep being dependable and trustworthy!

8. **Empathy**: Your empathy towards students is heartwarming. You provide support and understanding when they need it most. Keep being compassionate!

9. **Organizational Skills**: Your organizational skills are excellent. You help keep the classroom running smoothly and efficiently. Keep up the great organization!

10. **Patience**: Your patience with students is commendable. You give them the time and support they need to succeed, especially those with IEPs. Keep being patient and understanding!

11. **Problem-Solving**: Your problem-solving abilities are impressive. You assist in tackling challenges with creativity and persistence. Keep enhancing those skills!

12. **Positive Attitude**: Your positive attitude is infectious. You create a cheerful and motivating environment for students. Keep spreading that positivity!

13. **Student Support**: Your support for students is invaluable. You help them overcome obstacles and achieve their goals

under the teacher's guidance. Keep being a supportive mentor!

14. **Resourcefulness**: Your resourcefulness in finding solutions is impressive. You always find a way to make things work for students and teachers. Keep being resourceful!

15. **Flexibility**: Your flexibility in handling different tasks is commendable. You adapt quickly and effectively to any situation in the classroom. Keep being flexible!

16. **Encouragement**: Your encouragement boosts students' confidence. You make them believe in their abilities and strive for success. Keep being their cheerleader!

17. **Attention to Detail**: Your attention to detail ensures high-quality work. You catch the small things that make a big difference in students' learning. Keep being meticulous!

18. **Conflict Resolution**: Your conflict resolution skills are outstanding. You handle disputes calmly and fairly, helping maintain peace in the classroom and on the playground. Thank you for being a peacemaker!

19. **Dedication**: Your dedication to your role is truly admirable. You put in the effort and go above and beyond to support students and teachers. Thank you for your passion and dedication!

20. **Initiative**: Your initiative in taking on new tasks is impressive. You see what needs to be done and do it without waiting to be asked. I truly appreciate your initiative!

21. **Multitasking**: Your ability to multitask is remarkable. You handle multiple responsibilities efficiently, supporting both students and teachers. You are the King/Queen of Juggling!

22. **Cultural Sensitivity**: Your cultural sensitivity is com-

mendable. You respect and celebrate diversity in the classroom. Continue fostering inclusivity!

23. **Time Management**: Your time management skills are excellent. You make the most of every minute to support student learning. Thank you for this mastery!

24. **Student Relationships**: Your rapport with students is fantastic. They trust and look up to you as a valuable support figure. Keep building those positive relationships!

25. **Team Support**: Your support for the teaching team is invaluable. You contribute significantly to our collective success by working closely with teachers. You're a great team player!

26. **Tech Savvy**: Your proficiency with technology is impressive. You help integrate tech into learning seamlessly, enhancing the educational experience.

27. **Initiative**: Your initiative in taking on new tasks is impressive. You see what needs to be done and do it without waiting to be asked.

28. **Student Assessment**: Your skills in assisting with student assessments are remarkable. You help identify areas for improvement and support their growth. I know everyone appreciates your insightfulness.

29. **Health and Safety**: Your attention to health and safety protocols is commendable. You ensure a safe environment for students to learn and thrive. Thank you for prioritizing safety!

30. **Motivation**: Your ability to motivate students is exceptional. You inspire them to do their best through your supportive presence. Keep being a motivational force!

31. **Professional Development**: Your commitment to professional development is impressive. You continuously

seek to improve and grow in your role. Keep learning and evolving!

32. **Calm Under Pressure**: Your calm demeanor under pressure is admirable. You handle stressful situations with grace, supporting students effectively. Thank you for your composure.

33. **Inclusivity**: Your efforts to include all students are outstanding. You ensure everyone feels valued and included in the learning process. Thank you for championing inclusivity!

34. **Instructional Support**: Your instructional support is invaluable. You help clarify and reinforce learning concepts under the teacher's direction. Thank you for providing that essential support!

35. **Student Advocacy**: Your advocacy for students is inspiring. You ensure their voices are heard and needs met, especially those with IEPs. Keep being their advocate!

36. **Passion**: Your passion for education is evident in all you do. You inspire both students and colleagues alike with your dedication. Keep fueling that passion!

37. **Goal Setting**: Your help in setting and achieving goals with students is commendable. You guide them towards success with clear objectives.

38. **Resource Coordination**: Your coordination of resources is impressive. You ensure materials and tools are available and organized for effective learning. Thank you for managing our resources so well!

39. **Volunteer Efforts**: Your volunteer efforts beyond the classroom are truly appreciated. You give your time generously to various school activities. Everyone really appreciates your involvement!

40. **Feedback**: Your constructive feedback helps students improve continuously. You provide guidance with kindness and clarity. Keep giving that valuable feedback!

41. **Classroom Atmosphere**: Your contributions to a positive classroom atmosphere are invaluable. You create a welcoming and encouraging space for learning. Keep fostering that environment!

42. **Mentorship**: Your mentorship to new staff is commendable. You help them adjust and excel in their roles as paraprofessionals. Keep being a great mentor!

43. **Positive Reinforcement**: Your use of positive reinforcement is highly effective. You encourage good behavior and academic effort through your supportive approach.

44. **Individual Attention**: Your ability to give individual attention to students is impressive. You make each student feel valued and supported, especially those with special needs. Thank you for being so attentive!

45. **Conflict Mediation**: Your mediation skills are top-notch. You help resolve conflicts peacefully and fairly among students.

46. **Listening Skills**: Your listening skills are exceptional. You hear and understand the needs and concerns of students and staff, providing valuable support. You're a great listener!

47. **Energy and Enthusiasm**: Your energy and enthusiasm are contagious. You bring a vibrant spirit to the classroom, motivating students to learn. Keep spreading that enthusiasm!

48. **Adaptation to Feedback**: Your ability to adapt to feedback is impressive. You use it to improve and grow continuously in your role. I appreciate how open you

are to growth!

49. **Professionalism**: Your professionalism sets a great example. You conduct yourself with integrity and respect, earning the trust of students and staff. Keep being a professional role model!

50. **Resourcefulness**: Your resourcefulness in finding solutions is impressive. You always find a way to make things work, supporting students and teachers effectively. Thank you for being so resourceful!

STAFF

Words of praise from the administrator to the school staff are a tribute to their steadfast dedication and hard work. These acknowledgments underscore that their efforts are deeply valued. While faculty often take center stage, the staff's invaluable contributions form the backbone of the school's operations, ensuring everything runs seamlessly. Their exceptional support and commitment deserve sincere recognition.

1. **Janitorial Excellence**: Your dedication to keeping our school clean and safe is outstanding. You ensure every classroom and hallway is spotless. Thank you for creating a welcoming environment!

2. **Cafeteria Kindness**: Your friendly demeanor in the cafeteria brightens every student's day. You serve nutritious meals with a smile. Thank you for making lunchtime enjoyable!

3. **Office Efficiency**: Your efficiency in the office keeps everything running smoothly. You handle every task with precision and care. Thank you for your exceptional organizational skills!

4. **Secretarial Support**: Your support as a secretary is

invaluable. You manage schedules, communications and countless details flawlessly. Thank you for keeping us on track!

5. **Clerical Coordination**: Your coordination as a clerk ensures everything is in order. You handle paperwork and administrative tasks with ease. Thank you for your meticulous attention to detail!

6. **Nursing Care**: Your care as a school nurse is a lifeline for students. You provide medical attention and emotional support with compassion. Thank you for keeping our students healthy!

7. **Counseling Guidance**: Your guidance as a counselor helps students navigate challenges. You offer a listening ear and wise advice. Thank you for your unwavering support!

8. **Reception Warmth**: Your warmth at the reception desk creates a welcoming first impression. You greet everyone with kindness and professionalism. Thank you for your friendly presence!

9. **Maintenance Diligence**: Your diligence in maintenance ensures our facilities are in top condition. You handle repairs and upkeep promptly and efficiently. Thank you for your attention to all the details that keep the school running smoothly!

10. **Food Preparation**: Your care in preparing meals in the cafeteria is evident. You ensure that every student receives a nutritious lunch. Thank you for your dedication to their well-being!

11. **Administrative Support**: Your support in administrative tasks is crucial. You help keep the school running smoothly with your efficient work. Thank you for your valuable

contributions!

12. **Transportation Coordination**: Your coordination of transportation ensures students arrive safely. You manage bus schedules and routes with precision. Thank you for your careful planning!

13. **Library Assistance**: Your assistance in the library fosters a love of reading. You help students find the books they need and maintain a quiet study environment. Thank you for supporting literacy!

14. **Tech Support**: Your technical support keeps our systems running smoothly. You solve IT issues quickly and effectively. Thank you for ensuring our technology works flawlessly!

15. **Resource Management**: Your management of resources ensures we have what we need. You keep supplies organized and accessible. Thank you for your excellent stewardship!

16. **Attendance Tracking**: Your accuracy in tracking attendance is vital. You ensure records are up-to-date and correct. Thank you for your meticulous record-keeping!

17. **Event Planning**: Your planning of school events makes every occasion special. You coordinate details and ensure everything runs smoothly. Thank you for your event expertise!

18. **Health Education**: Your education on health topics helps students make informed choices. You provide valuable information and support. Thank you for promoting health and wellness!

19. **Behavioral Support**: Your support in managing student behavior is essential. You handle situations with patience and understanding. Thank you for your skillful guidance!

20. **Safety Oversight**: Your oversight ensures our school is a safe place. You monitor and enforce safety protocols diligently. Thank you for your commitment to safety!

21. **Cafeteria Cleanliness**: Your efforts in maintaining cafeteria cleanliness are impressive. You ensure a hygienic environment for students to eat. Thank you for your attention to detail!

22. **Records Management**: Your management of school records is impeccable. You keep important documents organized and accessible. Thank you for your efficient handling of information!

23. **Student Support**: Your support of students in various roles is invaluable. You offer assistance and encouragement daily. Thank you for being a dependable ally!

24. **Facilities Management**: Your management of facilities ensures everything is in top shape. You oversee maintenance and improvements diligently. Thank you for your hard work!

25. **Parental Communication**: Your communication with parents keeps them informed and engaged. You handle inquiries and updates professionally. Thank you for your excellent communication skills!

26. **Scheduling Expertise**: Your expertise in scheduling ensures everything runs smoothly. You coordinate events, meetings and classes seamlessly. Thank you for your organizational prowess!

27. **Community Outreach**: Your outreach efforts strengthen our connection with the community. You engage with local organizations and parents effectively. Thank you for fostering strong relationships!

28. **Emergency Response**: Your quick response in emer-

gencies is crucial. You handle crises with calm and competence. Thank you for your reliable presence in critical times!

29. **Counseling Support**: Your support as a counselor helps students thrive. You provide guidance and care that make a significant impact. Thank you for your dedication to their well-being!

30. **Volunteer Coordination**: Your coordination of volunteers enhances our school. You manage schedules and tasks efficiently. Thank you for organizing our valuable helpers!

31. **Student Advocacy**: Your advocacy for students ensures their needs are met. You speak up on their behalf and provide essential support. Thank you for championing their success!

32. **Health Monitoring**: Your monitoring of student health is vital. You keep track of medical needs and provide necessary care. Thank you for your attention to their well-being!

33. **Visitor Management**: Your management of visitors ensures our school remains secure. You handle check-ins and inquiries professionally. Thank you for maintaining a safe environment!

34. **Budget Management**: Your management of the school budget is outstanding. You ensure resources are used wisely and effectively. Thank you for your financial stewardship!

35. **Team Coordination**: Your coordination of staff teams enhances our operations. You facilitate collaboration and communication effectively. Thank you for your leadership!

36. **Academic Support**: Your support of academic programs is invaluable. You assist with various tasks that enhance student learning. Thank you for your dedication to education!

37. **Conflict Resolution**: Your resolution of conflicts is exemplary. You handle disputes fairly and professionally. Thank you for maintaining harmony!

38. **Custodial Care**: Your care in custodial duties ensures our school is always clean and welcoming. You work diligently to maintain high standards. Thank you for your hard work!

39. **Lunch Supervision**: Your supervision during lunch periods keeps students safe and orderly. You manage the cafeteria with skill and care. Thank you for your vigilance!

40. **Administrative Efficiency**: Your efficiency in administrative tasks keeps everything on track. You handle multiple responsibilities with ease. Thank you for your exceptional work!

41. **Student Mentorship**: Your mentorship of students provides valuable guidance. You help them navigate challenges and achieve their goals. Thank you for being a trusted mentor!

42. **Supplies Management**: Your management of supplies ensures we have what we need. You keep track of inventory and distribute materials efficiently. Thank you for your careful oversight!

43. **Health and Wellness Programs**: Your coordination of health and wellness programs benefits our students. You provide valuable resources and support. Thank you for promoting healthy habits!

44. **Extracurricular Support**: Your support of extracurricu-

lar activities enriches student life. You help organize and manage various programs. Thank you for enhancing our school community!

45. **School Spirit**: Your enthusiasm for fostering school spirit is contagious. You help create a positive and vibrant atmosphere. Thank you for boosting morale!

46. **Clerical Accuracy**: Your accuracy in clerical work ensures everything runs smoothly. You handle data and records with precision. Thank you for your meticulous work!

47. **Cafeteria Teamwork**: Your teamwork in the cafeteria ensures efficient meal service. You work well with colleagues to meet students' needs. Thank you for your collaborative spirit!

48. **First Aid Skills**: Your first aid skills provide essential care when needed. You handle medical situations with expertise and compassion. Thank you for keeping our students safe!

49. **Event Logistics**: Your handling of event logistics ensures everything runs smoothly. You manage details and coordination with precision. Thank you for your exceptional organizational skills!

50. **Resource Accessibility**: Your efforts in making resources accessible to students are commendable. You ensure they have the materials they need to succeed. Thank you for your support and dedication!

VOLUNTEERS

Words of gratitude from the administrator to school volunteers are a heartfelt tribute to their invaluable dedication and contributions. These expressions of appreciation emphasize how deeply their efforts are valued. While teachers and staff play crucial roles, volunteers' diverse contributions enrich every aspect of the school community. Whether assisting in classrooms, organizing events or providing essential support behind the scenes, their untiring commitment ensures that the school thrives. Their selfless service and dedication truly deserve your sincere recognition and thanks.

1. **Commitment**: Your untiring commitment to volunteering at our school is truly inspiring. Your dedication has made a significant impact on both students and staff. Thank you for your time and for being so dependable and generous!
2. **Event Support**: Your support at school events is invaluable. You ensure everything runs smoothly and everyone feels welcome. Thank you for your hard work and cheerful presence!
3. **Reading Assistance**: Your help with our reading pro-

grams has greatly benefited our students. You make reading fun and accessible, fostering a love for books. Thank you for your patience and enthusiasm!

4. **Classroom Aid**: Your assistance in the classroom helps create a supportive learning environment. You provide essential support to both teachers and students. Thank you for being such a reliable classroom aid!

5. **Fundraising Efforts**: Your efforts in organizing fundraisers have significantly contributed to our school's resources. Your creativity and hard work are deeply appreciated. Thank you for your dedication to our cause!

6. **Tutoring**: Your one-on-one tutoring sessions have helped many students improve their academic skills. Your patience and personalized attention make a huge difference. Thank you for your commitment to student success!

7. **Arts and Crafts**: Your contributions to our arts and crafts programs bring joy and creativity to our students. You inspire them to express themselves artistically. Thank you for sharing your talent and enthusiasm!

8. **Library Support**: Your help in the library has made it a more organized and welcoming place. Students benefit from your dedication to keeping everything in order. Thank you for your meticulous work!

9. **Sports Coaching**: Your volunteer coaching has fostered teamwork and sportsmanship among our students. You bring out the best in them on and off the field. Thank you for your inspiring leadership!

10. **Administrative Assistance**: Your support with administrative tasks helps our school run more smoothly. Your efficiency and attention to detail are greatly appreciated. Thank you for your invaluable help!

11. **Field Trip Chaperone**: Your willingness to chaperone field trips ensures our students have safe and enriching experiences. Your presence and guidance make these trips memorable. Thank you for your dedication!

12. **Mentoring**: Your mentoring has provided guidance and support to many students. Your wisdom and encouragement help them navigate their challenges. Thank you for being a positive role model!

13. **Tech Support**: Your assistance with technology has been crucial. You help troubleshoot issues and teach students valuable tech skills. Thank you for your technical expertise!

14. **Parent Communication**: Your help with parent communications keeps everyone informed and engaged. Your efforts strengthen our school community. Thank you for your effective communication skills!

15. **Community Outreach**: Your outreach efforts help connect our school with the wider community. You build relationships that benefit our students and programs. Thank you for your community spirit!

16. **Garden Projects**: Your work in the school garden teaches students about nature and sustainability. Your green thumb and dedication are evident in every plant. Thank you for nurturing both our students and our garden!

17. **Language Support**: Your language skills help bridge communication gaps for non-English speaking families. You provide essential support and inclusion. Thank you for your linguistic expertise!

18. **Safety Patrol**: Your vigilance on safety patrol ensures our students are safe during arrival and departure times. Your presence is reassuring to both parents and staff. Thank

you for keeping our students safe!

19. **Lunchroom Help**: Your assistance in the lunchroom makes mealtime smoother for everyone. You ensure students are well-fed and happy. Thank you for your caring and efficient service!

20. **Special Projects**: Your involvement in special projects brings fresh ideas and energy to our school. You help make our initiatives successful and impactful. Thank you for your creativity and hard work!

21. **Holiday Celebrations**: Your help with holiday celebrations brings joy and festivity to our school. You make these occasions special for students and staff alike. Thank you for spreading holiday cheer!

22. **Music Programs**: Your contributions to our music programs inspire students to explore their musical talents. You help create a vibrant and dynamic learning environment. Thank you for sharing your passion for music!

23. **Homework Club**: Your support in the homework club ensures students have the help they need to succeed. Your patience and encouragement make a big difference. Thank you for your dedication!

24. **Health and Wellness**: Your efforts in promoting health and wellness are greatly appreciated. You provide valuable resources and support for our students' well-being. Thank you for your commitment to health education!

25. **School Beautification**: Your work on beautification projects enhances our school environment. You create a more pleasant and inspiring place for everyone. Thank you for your artistic vision and hard work!

26. **Alumni Relations**: Your efforts in maintaining connections with alumni strengthen our school community. You

help create a lasting legacy for our institution. Thank you for your dedication to alumni relations!

27. **Drama Club**: Your support of the drama club brings out students' creativity and confidence. You help make productions successful and enjoyable. Thank you for your enthusiasm and expertise!

28. **Book Fairs**: Your organization of book fairs promotes literacy and a love of reading. You make these events enjoyable and beneficial for everyone. Thank you for your hard work and passion!

29. **Cultural Programs**: Your involvement in cultural programs enriches our students' learning experiences. You help celebrate and educate about diverse cultures. Thank you for your dedication to cultural enrichment!

30. **Science Experiments**: Your help with science experiments makes learning hands-on and exciting. You bring a sense of wonder and curiosity to the classroom. Thank you for fostering a love of science!

31. **Peer Mediation**: Your work with peer mediation programs helps resolve conflicts and build a positive school climate. You teach students valuable conflict resolution skills. Thank you for your dedication to harmony!

32. **Social Media Management**: Your management of our school's social media keeps our community informed and engaged. You highlight our achievements and events effectively. Thank you for your digital expertise!

33. **Snack Program**: Your support in the snack program ensures students have healthy options throughout the day. Your efforts contribute to their overall well-being. Thank you for your commitment to student health!

34. **Library Storytime**: Your storytelling sessions in the

library captivate and inspire young readers. You bring stories to life with your engaging presentations. Thank you for sharing your love of literature!

35. **Career Day**: Your organization of career day events provides students with valuable insights into various professions. You help broaden their horizons and inspire their futures. Thank you for your dedication to career education!

36. **Art Program Support**: Your assistance in the art program nurtures students' creativity and self-expression. You help create a vibrant and dynamic learning environment. Thank you for your artistic guidance!

37. **Emergency Preparedness**: Your work on emergency preparedness ensures our school is ready for any situation. You help keep students and staff safe. Thank you for your attention to safety!

38. **After-School Programs**: Your involvement in after-school programs provides students with enriching activities and support. You create a safe and engaging environment for learning and fun. Thank you for your dedication!

39. **Playground Supervision**: Your supervision on the playground ensures students have a safe and enjoyable time. You help prevent accidents and encourage positive play. Thank you for your vigilant care!

40. **School Tours**: Your guidance on school tours provides visitors with a welcoming and informative experience. You represent our school with pride and professionalism. Thank you for being an excellent ambassador!

41. **Special Needs Support**: Your support for special needs students is invaluable. You provide individualized atten-

tion and care that helps them thrive. Thank you for your compassion and dedication!

42. **Bulletin Boards**: Your creative bulletin board displays make our hallways vibrant and informative. You highlight important information and celebrate student achievements. Thank you for your artistic contributions!

43. **Parent-Teacher Association**: Your active involvement in the PTA strengthens our school community. You help organize events and initiatives that benefit everyone. Thank you for your leadership and commitment!

44. **Technology Integration**: Your assistance with integrating technology into the classroom enhances learning experiences. You help students and teachers navigate new tools and resources. Thank you for your tech support!

45. **Cultural Celebrations**: Your organization of cultural celebrations fosters inclusivity and understanding. You help create an environment that respects and values diversity. Thank you for promoting cultural awareness!

46. **Green Initiatives**: Your efforts in promoting green initiatives help our school become more environmentally friendly. You educate and inspire students to care for our planet. Thank you for your eco-friendly contributions!

47. **Yearbook Production**: Your work on the yearbook captures the memories and milestones of our school year. You create a treasured keepsake for students and staff. Thank you for your dedication to preserving our history!

48. **Parent Workshops**: Your organization of parent workshops provides valuable resources and support for families. You help build a stronger, more connected school community. Thank you for your commitment to parent education!

49. **Holiday Gift Drives**: Your efforts in organizing holiday gift drives bring joy to many families. You help ensure that everyone has a happy holiday season. Thank you for your generosity and compassion!

50. **Volunteer Recruitment**: Your recruitment and coordination of volunteers enhance our school programs and events. You bring together a dedicated team to support our students and staff. Thank you for your exceptional organizational skills!

SCHOOL BOARD

Words of gratitude from the administrator on behalf of the school to a school board and its members are a recognition of their tireless dedication and leadership. These expressions of appreciation highlight the profound value of their efforts. Their strategic guidance and unwavering commitment to the school steer the institution forward, ensuring excellence in education.

1. **Visionary Leadership:** Your visionary leadership has paved the way for our school's success. We appreciate your steadfast support and commitment. Thank you for guiding us towards excellence.
2. **Time and Effort:** The time and effort you invest in our school make a significant difference. Your guidance has been invaluable to our success. We are grateful for your steadfast support.
3. **High Standards:** Your leadership has set a high standard for our entire community. Thank you for your tireless efforts and insightful direction. We are fortunate to have you on our board.
4. **Passion for Education:** The passion you bring to our school board is palpable. Your commitment to education

is deeply appreciated. Thank you for your unwavering dedication and support.

5. **Strategic Vision:** Your strategic vision has been a driving force behind our school's achievements. We are grateful for your thoughtful leadership. Thank you for your endless commitment to our success.

6. **Invaluable Contributions:** Your contributions to our school are immeasurable. We deeply appreciate your time, effort and leadership. Thank you for your unwavering dedication.

7. **Beacon of Guidance:** Your guidance has been a beacon of light for our school. We are grateful for your steadfast leadership and support. Thank you for always putting our students first.

8. **Commitment to Values:** Your commitment to our school's values is evident in all that you do. We appreciate your tireless efforts and dedication. Thank you for being a guiding force in our community.

9. **Unnoticed Efforts:** The countless hours you dedicate to our school board do not go unnoticed. Your leadership has made a significant impact on our students and staff. Thank you for your untiring support.

10. **Instrumental Leadership:** Your vision and leadership have been instrumental in our school's success. We appreciate your commitment and dedication. Thank you for guiding us towards a brighter future.

11. **Shining Passion:** Your passion for education shines through in your work on the school board. We are grateful for your unwavering commitment. Thank you for your thoughtful leadership and support.

12. **Positive Environment:** Your efforts have created a

positive and thriving environment for our school. We deeply appreciate your time and dedication. Thank you for your insightful guidance.

13. **Cornerstone of Success:** Your leadership has been a cornerstone of our school's success. We are grateful for your tireless efforts and steadfast support. Thank you for your dedication.

14. **Inspired Excellence:** Your commitment to excellence has inspired our entire school community. We appreciate your leadership and guidance. Thank you for your tireless support.

15. **Significant Impact:** Your thoughtful decisions have significantly impacted our school's growth and success. We are grateful for your expertise and involvement. Thank you for leading us with such grace.

16. **Commendable Dedication:** Your dedication to our school's mission is truly commendable. We appreciate your resolute support and visionary leadership. Thank you for guiding us towards excellence.

17. **Valuable Guidance:** The time and effort you invest in our school make a significant difference. Your guidance has been invaluable to our success. We are grateful for your steadfast support.

18. **High Community Standards:** Your leadership has set a high standard for our entire community. Thank you for your tireless efforts and insightful direction. We are fortunate to have you on our board.

19. **Educational Passion:** The passion you bring to our school board is palpable. Your commitment to education is deeply appreciated. Thank you for your unwavering dedication and support.

20. **Driving Achievements:** Your strategic vision has been a driving force behind our school's achievements. We are grateful for your thoughtful leadership. Thank you for your endless commitment to our success.

21. **Immeasurable Contributions:** Your contributions to our school are immeasurable. We deeply appreciate your time, effort and leadership. Thank you for your dedication.

22. **Steadfast Guidance:** Your guidance has been a beacon of light for our school. We are grateful for your steadfast leadership and support. Thank you for always putting our students first.

23. **Values Commitment:** Your commitment to our school's values is evident in all that you do. We appreciate your tireless efforts and dedication. Thank you for being a guiding force in our community.

24. **Unnoticed Dedication:** The countless hours you dedicate to our school board do not go unnoticed. Your leadership has made a significant impact on our students and staff. Thank you for your unwavering support.

25. **Instrumental Vision:** Your vision and leadership have been instrumental in our school's success. We appreciate your commitment and dedication. Thank you for guiding us towards a brighter future.

26. **Shining Commitment:** Your passion for education shines through in your work on the school board. We are grateful for your untiring commitment. Thank you for your thoughtful leadership and support.

27. **Thriving Environment:** Your efforts have created a positive and thriving environment for our school. We deeply appreciate your time and dedication. Thank you

for your insightful guidance.

28. **Success Cornerstone:** Your leadership has been a cornerstone of our school's success. We are grateful for your tireless efforts and unwavering support. Thank you for your dedication.

29 **Inspired Leadership:** Your commitment to excellence has inspired our entire school community. We appreciate your leadership and guidance. Thank you for your unswerving support.

30. **Significant Decisions:** Your thoughtful decisions have significantly impacted our school's growth and success. We are grateful for your expertise and involvement. Thank you for leading us with such grace.

31. **Commendable Mission:** Your dedication to our school's mission is truly commendable. We appreciate your unwavering support and visionary leadership. Thank you for guiding us towards excellence.

32. **Invaluable Investment:** The time and effort you invest in our school make a significant difference. Your guidance has been invaluable to our success. We are grateful for your steadfast support.

33. **Community Standards:** Your leadership has set a high standard for our entire community. Thank you for your tireless efforts and insightful direction. We are fortunate to have you on our board.

34. **Palpable Passion:** The passion you bring to our school board is palpable. Your commitment to education is deeply appreciated. Thank you for your unwavering dedication and support.

35. **Driving Vision:** Your strategic vision has been a driving force behind our school's achievements. We are grateful

for your thoughtful leadership. Thank you for your endless commitment to our success.

36. **Unmeasured Contributions:** Your contributions to our school are immeasurable. We deeply appreciate your time, effort and leadership. Thank you for your unwavering dedication.

37. **Steadfast Beacon:** Your guidance has been a beacon of light for our school. We are grateful for your steadfast leadership and support. Thank you for always putting our students first.

38. **Commitment to Values:** Your commitment to our school's values is evident in all that you do. We appreciate your tireless efforts and dedication. Thank you for being a guiding force in our community.

39. **Unseen Efforts:** The countless hours you dedicate to our school board do not go unnoticed. Your leadership has made a significant impact on our students and staff. Thank you for your unwavering support.

40. **Bright Vision:** Your vision and leadership have been instrumental in our school's success. We appreciate your commitment and dedication. Thank you for guiding us towards a brighter future.

41. **Shining Education:** Your passion for education shines through in your work on the school board. We are grateful for your unwavering commitment. Thank you for your thoughtful leadership and support.

42. **Thriving Efforts:** Your efforts have created a positive and thriving environment for our school. We deeply appreciate your time and dedication. Thank you for your insightful guidance.

43. **Success Foundation:** Your leadership has been a corner-

stone of our school's success. We are grateful for your tireless efforts and unwavering support. Thank you for your dedication.

44. **Inspiring Excellence:** Your commitment to excellence has inspired our entire school community. We appreciate your leadership and guidance. Thank you for your unwavering support.

45. **Impactful Decisions:** Your thoughtful decisions have significantly impacted our school's growth and success. We are grateful for your expertise and involvement. Thank you for leading us with such grace.

46. **Mission Dedication:** Your dedication to our school's mission is truly commendable. We appreciate your unwavering support and visionary leadership. Thank you for guiding us towards excellence.

47. **Significant Time:** The time and effort you invest in our school make a significant difference. Your guidance has been invaluable to our success. We are grateful for your steadfast support.

48. **High Leadership:** Your leadership has set a high standard for our entire community. Thank you for your tireless efforts and insightful direction. We are fortunate to have you on our board.

49. **Education Passion:** The passion you bring to our school board is palpable. Your commitment to education is deeply appreciated. Thank you for your unwavering dedication and support.

50. **Achievement Vision:** Your strategic vision has been a driving force behind our school's achievements. We are grateful for your thoughtful leadership. Thank you for your endless commitment to our success.

ADMINISTRATIVE LEADERSHIP

S chool administrators include various roles that support school operations. From the vice principal to the school psychologist, middle school director to the business manager, these administrative leaders direct the various working parts of a successful school. Here are the right words when well-deserved kudos from the head administrator on behalf of the school are needed.

1. **Visionary Leadership:** Your visionary leadership has been instrumental in driving our school's success. We appreciate your foresight and strategic planning. Thank you for always leading with integrity and purpose.
2. **Innovative Approaches:** Your innovative approaches to education have transformed our school environment. We admire your creativity and dedication to continuous improvement. Thank you for always pushing the boundaries to enhance student learning.
3. **Inspirational Guidance:** Your inspirational guidance has motivated both staff and students to strive for excellence. We appreciate your unwavering support and encouragement. Thank you for being a source of strength and inspiration.

4. **Commitment to Excellence:** Your commitment to excellence sets a high standard for everyone at our school. We are grateful for your dedication and hard work. Thank you for always aiming for the best.

5. **Supportive Leadership:** Your supportive leadership has fostered a collaborative and positive work environment. We appreciate your willingness to listen and help whenever needed. Thank you for being a pillar of support.

6. **Effective Communication:** Your effective communication skills have ensured that everyone is on the same page. We value your transparency and clarity in conveying information. Thank you for keeping us well-informed and connected.

7. **Problem-Solving Skills:** Your exceptional problem-solving skills have helped us navigate through challenges with ease. We appreciate your ability to find practical solutions. Thank you for being a reliable and resourceful leader.

8. **Passion for Education:** Your passion for education is evident in everything you do. We admire your dedication to nurturing young minds. Thank you for your tireless efforts to make a difference in students' lives.

9. **Strategic Planning:** Your strategic planning has laid a strong foundation for our school's growth and development. We appreciate your foresight and meticulous attention to detail. Thank you for guiding us towards a brighter future.

10. **Empowering Leadership:** Your empowering leadership has enabled us to reach our full potential. We value your trust and confidence in our abilities. Thank you for always encouraging us to excel.

11. **Dedication to Student Success:** Your dedication to student success has been truly inspiring. We appreciate your unwavering focus on their well-being and academic growth. Thank you for putting students at the heart of everything you do.

12. **Building Strong Relationships:** Your ability to build strong relationships has created a supportive and inclusive school community. We admire your interpersonal skills and genuine care for others. Thank you for fostering a sense of belonging.

13. **Commitment to Professional Development:** Your commitment to professional development has helped us grow as educators. We appreciate the opportunities for learning and growth you provide. Thank you for investing in our development.

14. **Leading by Example:** Your practice of leading by example sets a powerful precedent for all of us. We admire your integrity and work ethic. Thank you for being a role model we can look up to.

15. **Focus on Innovation:** Your focus on innovation has kept our school at the forefront of educational advancements. We appreciate your willingness to embrace new ideas and technologies. Thank you for keeping us ahead of the curve.

16. **Positive Attitude:** Your positive attitude and optimism are contagious. We admire your ability to stay upbeat and motivate others. Thank you for bringing a sense of joy and enthusiasm to our school.

17. **Visionary Initiatives:** Your visionary initiatives have driven meaningful change in our school. We value your innovative ideas and strategic direction. Thank you for always looking ahead and planning for the future.

18. **Effective Decision-Making:** Your effective decision-making has steered us through both good times and challenges. We appreciate your ability to weigh options and choose the best course of action. Thank you for your sound judgment and leadership.

19. **Dedication to Staff Well-Being:** Your dedication to staff well-being has created a supportive and positive work environment. We appreciate your focus on our professional and personal growth. Thank you for always looking out for us.

20. **Commitment to Lifelong Learning:** Your commitment to lifelong learning inspires us to keep growing and evolving. We admire your pursuit of knowledge and professional development. Thank you for setting an example of continuous improvement.

21. **Strong Work Ethic:** Your strong work ethic is evident in everything you do. We appreciate your dedication and tireless efforts. Thank you for being a hardworking and dependable leader.

22. **Collaborative Leadership:** Your collaborative leadership style fosters teamwork and cooperation. We value your ability to bring people together and work towards common goals. Thank you for creating a sense of unity and collaboration.

23. **Focus on Student Engagement:** Your focus on student engagement has made learning more dynamic and interactive. We admire your dedication to creating meaningful educational experiences. Thank you for making learning exciting and relevant.

24. **Resilience in Leadership:** Your resilience in the face of challenges has been truly inspiring. We appreciate your

ability to stay strong and lead with confidence. Thank you for guiding us through difficult times with grace.

25. **Commitment to Community:** Your commitment to building strong community connections has enriched our school. We value your efforts to engage with parents, local organizations, and stakeholders. Thank you for fostering a sense of community and partnership.

26. **Mentorship and Guidance:** Your mentorship and guidance have been invaluable to our professional growth. We appreciate your willingness to share your knowledge and experience. Thank you for being a supportive and inspiring mentor.

27. **Vision for the Future:** Your vision for the future has set a clear and ambitious path for our school. We admire your forward-thinking and strategic planning. Thank you for leading us towards new horizons.

28. **Focus on Student Well-Being:** Your focus on student well-being has created a nurturing and supportive environment. We appreciate your efforts to address their emotional and social needs. Thank you for caring deeply about our students' overall well-being.

29. **Commitment to Academic Excellence:** Your commitment to academic excellence has raised the bar for our school. We value your dedication to high standards and rigorous education. Thank you for challenging us to achieve our best.

30. **Effective Leadership:** Your effective leadership has guided us through numerous achievements and milestones. We appreciate your ability to lead with clarity and purpose. Thank you for being a reliable and inspiring leader.

31. **Focus on Professional Development:** Your focus on professional development has empowered us to grow and succeed. We value the opportunities you provide for learning and advancement. Thank you for investing in our careers.

32. **Passionate Advocacy:** Your passionate advocacy for education has made a significant impact on our school. We admire your dedication to fighting for the best interests of our students and staff. Thank you for being a tireless advocate.

33. **Innovative Solutions:** Your innovative solutions have addressed challenges in creative and effective ways. We appreciate your ability to think outside the box. Thank you for bringing fresh perspectives to our school.

34. **Commitment to Transparency:** Your commitment to transparency has built trust and confidence within our school community. We value your openness and honesty. Thank you for keeping us informed and engaged.

35. **Focus on Student Achievement:** Your focus on student achievement has driven our academic success. We admire your dedication to helping every student reach their potential. Thank you for prioritizing student outcomes.

36. **Effective Team Leadership:** Your effective team leadership has brought out the best in all of us. We appreciate your ability to inspire collaboration and cooperation. Thank you for leading with teamwork and unity.

37. **Focus on Continuous Improvement:** Your focus on continuous improvement drives us to strive for better outcomes. We appreciate your commitment to evaluating and enhancing our practices. Thank you for leading with a mindset of growth and progress.

38. **Student-Centered Leadership:** Your student-centered leadership has prioritized our learners' needs. We admire your dedication to creating a supportive and engaging educational experience. Thank you for prioritizing our students' success.

39. **Commitment to Collaboration:** Your commitment to collaboration has fostered a strong sense of teamwork. We appreciate your efforts to bring us together to achieve common goals. Thank you for promoting a collaborative culture.

40. **Positive Leadership:** Your positive leadership has created a motivating and uplifting school environment. We admire your ability to inspire and energize others. Thank you for leading with positivity and enthusiasm.

41. **Focus on Educational Excellence:** Your focus on educational excellence has elevated our school's standards. We value your dedication to high-quality teaching and learning. Thank you for striving for the best in education.

42. **Empowering Educators:** Your empowering leadership has enabled educators to thrive and succeed. We appreciate your trust and support in our professional growth. Thank you for empowering us to be our best.

43. **Strong Vision:** Your strong vision for our school has guided us towards remarkable achievements. We admire your strategic direction and clarity of purpose. Thank you for leading with a clear and compelling vision.

44. **Commitment to Student Development:** Your commitment to student development has created well-rounded learners. We value your focus on both academic and personal growth. Thank you for nurturing the whole child.

45. **Focus on Quality Education:** Your focus on quality

education has set high standards for our school. We appreciate your dedication to providing the best learning experiences. Thank you for striving for educational excellence.

46. **Effective Change Management:** Your effective change management has guided us through transitions smoothly. We admire your ability to navigate and implement changes successfully. Thank you for leading us with adaptability and foresight.

47. **Commitment to Teacher Support:** Your commitment to teacher support has created a positive and productive work environment. We value your efforts to provide resources and encouragement. Thank you for being a strong advocate for educators.

48. **Dedication to School Improvement:** Your dedication to school improvement has driven our continuous progress. We appreciate your focus on enhancing our practices and outcomes. Thank you for leading with a commitment to excellence.

VENDORS

The contributions of various vendors that provide services and products to the school are invaluable. From supplying educational materials and technology solutions to maintaining school facilities and providing nutritious meals, these vendors play a crucial role in supporting students, teachers and staff. Their dedication ensures that the classrooms are equipped with the latest resources, the facilities are well-maintained and safe, and the students have access to nutritious meals for their health and well-being. These words of appreciation from the administrator on behalf of the school go a long way to let them know you recognize the difference they make.

1. **Dedicated Custodial Services:** Your dedicated custodial services ensure our school is clean and safe every day. We appreciate your hard work and attention to detail. Thank you for maintaining a welcoming environment for our students and staff.

2. **Reliable Food Services:** Your reliable food services provide nutritious meals that fuel our students' learning. We appreciate your commitment to quality and freshness. Thank you for keeping our cafeteria running smoothly.

3. **Prompt Transportation Services:** Your prompt trans-portation services ensure our students arrive safely and on time. We appreciate your dedication to their safety and comfort. Thank you for being a reliable partner in student transportation.

4. **Efficient IT Support:** Your efficient IT support keeps our technology running smoothly, enhancing learning experi-ences. We appreciate your quick response to tech issues. Thank you for keeping us connected and productive.

5. **Quality Curriculum Providers:** Your quality curricu-lum resources enrich our teaching and learning experi-ences. We appreciate your commitment to educational excellence. Thank you for equipping us with tools to inspire our students.

6. **Responsive Maintenance Services:** Your responsive maintenance services keep our facilities in top shape for learning. We appreciate your timely repairs and upkeep. Thank you for ensuring a conducive environment for education.

7. **Supportive Counseling Services:** Your supportive coun-seling services provide crucial support to our students' emotional well-being. We appreciate your compassionate guidance and expertise. Thank you for helping our students thrive.

8. **Effective Security Services:** Your effective security services keep our school community safe and secure. We appreciate your vigilance and professionalism. Thank you for prioritizing our students' safety.

9. **Creative Extracurricular Providers:** Your creative extracurricular programs offer enriching activities outside the classroom. We appreciate your dedication to student

engagement. Thank you for broadening our students' horizons.

10. **Responsive Printing Services:** Your responsive printing services deliver timely materials that support our educational initiatives. We appreciate your attention to detail and quick turnaround. Thank you for helping us communicate effectively.

11. **Innovative Educational Technology Providers:** Your innovative educational technology solutions enhance our teaching methods and student learning outcomes. We appreciate your commitment to advancing education through technology. Thank you for keeping us at the forefront of digital learning.

12. **Supportive Special Education Services:** Your support ensures all students receive the tailored support they need. We appreciate your dedication to inclusive education. Thank you for making a difference in the lives of our students.

13. **Collaborative Professional Development Providers:** Your collaborative professional development programs empower our staff with new skills and knowledge. We appreciate your commitment to enhancing educator effectiveness. Thank you for investing in our professional growth.

14. **Comprehensive Insurance Services:** Your comprehensive insurance services provide peace of mind for our school community. We appreciate your thorough coverage and support. Thank you for protecting our school's interests.

15. **Innovative STEM Program Providers:** Your innovative STEM programs inspire curiosity and critical thinking

among our students. We appreciate your dedication to STEM education. Thank you for preparing our students for future success.

16. **Engaging Guest Speakers:** Your engaging guest speakers bring valuable insights and inspiration to our students. We appreciate your contributions to their personal and academic growth. Thank you for broadening their perspectives.

17. **Professional Sports Coaching Services:** Your professional sports coaching services develop our students' athletic skills and teamwork abilities. We appreciate your commitment to sportsmanship and skill-building. Thank you for fostering a love for sports among our students.

18. **Environmental Sustainability Services:** Your environmental sustainability services promote eco-friendly practices within our school. We appreciate your efforts to reduce our carbon footprint. Thank you for teaching our students the importance of environmental stewardship.

19. **Interactive Science Lab Equipment Providers:** Your interactive science lab equipment enhances hands-on learning experiences for our students. We appreciate your commitment to science education. Thank you for making learning engaging and impactful.

20. **Efficient School Supply Vendors:** Your efficient school supply services ensure we have everything we need for a productive learning environment. We appreciate your reliability and customer service. Thank you for supporting our educational mission.

21. **Inspirational Arts Program Providers:** Your inspirational arts programs nurture creativity and self-expression among our students. We appreciate your dedication to arts

education. Thank you for enriching our school culture through the arts.

22. **Dependable Bookkeeping Services:** Your dependable bookkeeping services maintain our financial records with accuracy and transparency. We appreciate your attention to detail and fiscal responsibility. Thank you for ensuring our financial health.

23. **Responsive Parent Communication Tools:** Your responsive parent communication tools facilitate strong partnerships between home and school. We appreciate your user-friendly platforms and support. Thank you for keeping parents informed and involved.

24. **Committed Volunteer Coordination Services:** Your committed volunteer coordination services recruit and organize invaluable support for our school events. We appreciate your dedication to community engagement. Thank you for enhancing our school programs through volunteerism.

25. **Innovative Playground Equipment Providers:** Your innovative playground equipment enhances physical activity and fun for our students. We appreciate your commitment to safe and engaging play environments. Thank you for promoting healthy lifestyles.

26. **Quality Language Learning Program Providers:** Your quality language learning programs broaden our students' linguistic skills and cultural awareness. We appreciate your dedication to global education. Thank you for preparing our students for a multicultural world.

27. **Efficient Waste Management Services:** Your efficient waste management services promote cleanliness and sustainability in our school. We appreciate your eco-friendly

practices and reliability. Thank you for keeping our campus clean and green.

28. **Educational Field Trip Organizers:** Your educational field trip planning services offer enriching experiences outside the classroom. We appreciate your attention to educational value and safety. Thank you for expanding our students' learning horizons.

29. **Supportive Mental Health Services:** Your supportive mental health services provide essential care and support to our students. We appreciate your dedication to their well-being. Thank you for promoting mental wellness in our school community.

30. **Comprehensive Facilities Management Services:** Your comprehensive facilities management services ensure our buildings are well-maintained and operational. We appreciate your proactive maintenance and responsive service. Thank you for creating a conducive learning environment.

31. **Engaging After-School Program Providers:** Your engaging after-school programs offer enriching activities for our students beyond the school day. We appreciate your commitment to their holistic development. Thank you for providing opportunities for growth and exploration.

32. **Reliable Bus Transportation Services:** Your reliable bus transportation services ensure our students arrive safely to and from school. We appreciate your adherence to schedules and safety protocols. Thank you for being a trusted partner in student transportation.

33. **Interactive Educational Software Providers:** Your interactive educational software enhances classroom learning experiences for our students. We appreciate your

innovative solutions and educational resources. Thank you for supporting our teaching efforts.

34. **Responsive Parent-Teacher Conference Tools:** Your responsive parent-teacher conference tools facilitate meaningful discussions about student progress. We appreciate your user-friendly platforms and support. Thank you for strengthening home-school partnerships.

35. **Engaging Music Program Providers:** Your engaging music programs inspire creativity and passion for music among our students. We appreciate your dedication to music education. Thank you for enriching our school community through music.

36. **Dependable Technology Maintenance Services:** Your dependable technology maintenance services keep our devices and networks running smoothly. We appreciate your expertise and quick response to tech issues. Thank you for supporting our digital learning environment.

37. **Supportive College Counseling Services:** Your supportive college counseling services guide our students through the college application process. We appreciate your expertise and individualized support. Thank you for helping our students achieve their academic goals.

38. **Innovative STEM Education Providers:** Your innovative STEM education programs inspire curiosity and critical thinking among our students. We appreciate your commitment to STEM learning. Thank you for preparing our students for future careers in science and technology.

39. **Responsive Athletic Equipment Providers:** Your responsive athletic equipment services ensure our sports teams have the gear they need to succeed. We appreciate your quality products and timely deliveries. Thank you

for supporting our student athletes.

40. **Creative School Photography Services:** Your creative school photography services capture memorable moments for our students and staff. We appreciate your artistic eye and professionalism. Thank you for preserving our school's memories.

41. **Efficient School Event Planning Services:** Your efficient school event planning services organize successful and memorable events for our school community. We appreciate your attention to detail and creativity. Thank you for making our events special.

42. **Supportive Speech Therapy Services:** Your supportive speech therapy services help our students improve their communication skills. We appreciate your dedication to their development. Thank you for making a difference in their lives.

43. **Committed Playground Supervision Services:** Your committed playground supervision services ensure our students play safely and responsibly. We appreciate your vigilance and care. Thank you for promoting active and healthy play.

44. **Inclusive Disability Services Providers:** Your inclusive disability services provide essential support to students with special needs. We appreciate your commitment to inclusive education. Thank you for creating opportunities for all students to thrive.

45. **Interactive Classroom Technology Providers:** Your interactive classroom technology enhances engagement and learning outcomes for our students. We appreciate your innovative solutions and support. Thank you for transforming our classrooms.

46. **Supportive Language Translation Services:** Your supportive language translation services facilitate communication with our diverse community. We appreciate your linguistic expertise and cultural sensitivity. Thank you for promoting inclusivity in our school.

47. **Quality Playground Maintenance Services:** Your quality playground maintenance services keep our play areas safe and enjoyable for our students. We appreciate your attention to detail and safety standards. Thank you for maintaining our outdoor spaces.

48. **Innovative Virtual Learning Platform Providers:** Your innovative virtual learning platforms support remote education and blended learning models. We appreciate your technological solutions and educational resources. Thank you for expanding our teaching capabilities.

COMPLIMENTARY CLOSE

The complimentary close is the word or phrase that usually appears before your signature in an email or a handwritten note. Here are 25 warm yet professional closes that a school administrator could use at the end of a note of appreciation. Each conveys a sense of professionalism while expressing genuine gratitude and appreciation. You may have your own signature close, but it's always nice to have options.

1. With deepest gratitude,
2. Sincerely appreciative,
3. With heartfelt thanks,
4. Gratefully yours,
5. With sincere thanks,
6. In appreciation,
7. With warm regards,
8. With my sincere gratitude,
9. Thank you for all you do,
10. With genuine thanks,
11. With great respect and thanks,
12. Appreciatively yours,
13. With heartfelt appreciation,
14. With sincere respect,

15. Warmest thanks,
16. In sincere appreciation,
17. With utmost gratitude,
18. With profound thanks,
19. Grateful for your support,
20. With sincere appreciation,
21. With a grateful heart,
22. With deepest respect,
23. With gratitude and best wishes,
24. With continued thanks,
25. Thank you for your dedication,

Made in the USA
Columbia, SC
10 October 2024

43392400R00039